EPIC MOVIE ADVENTURES
FOR EASY PIANO

ISBN 978-1-70516-367-2

Visit Hal Leonard Online at
www.halleonard.com

World headquarters, contact:
Hal Leonard
7777 West Bluemound Road
Milwaukee, WI 53213
Email: info@halleonard.com

In Europe, contact:
Hal Leonard Europe Limited
42 Wigmore Street
Marylebone, London, W1U 2RN
Email: info@halleonardeurope.com

In Australia, contact:
Hal Leonard Australia Pty. Ltd.
4 Lentara Court
Cheltenham, Victoria, 3192 Australia
Email: info@halleonard.com.au

ALL SYSTEMS GO

from APOLLO 13

Composed by
JAMES HORNER

Moderately

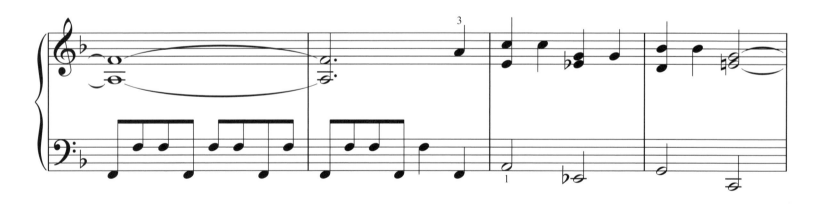

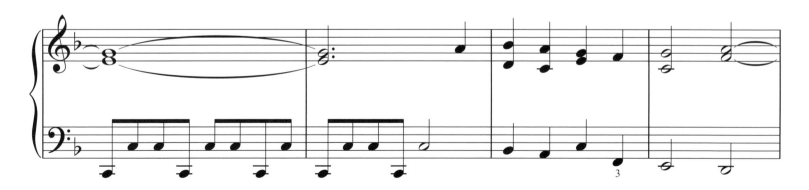

ALSO SPRACH ZARATHUSTRA, OPENING THEME

featured in the Motion Picture 2001: A SPACE ODYSSEY

By RICHARD STRAUSS

Moderately

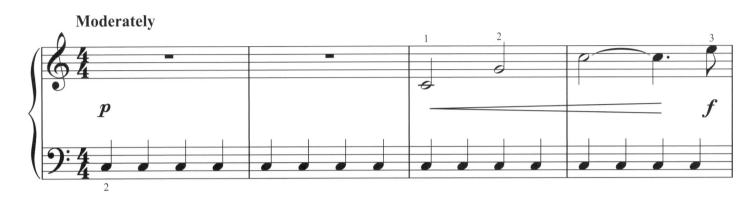

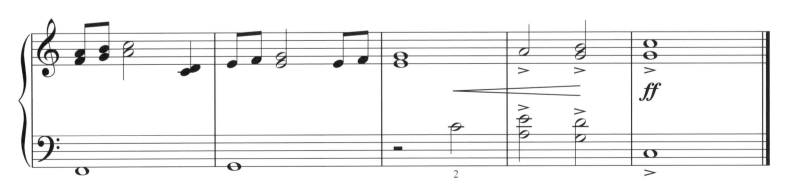

AVENGERS UNITE

from AVENGERS: AGE OF ULTRON

Music by DANNY ELFMAN

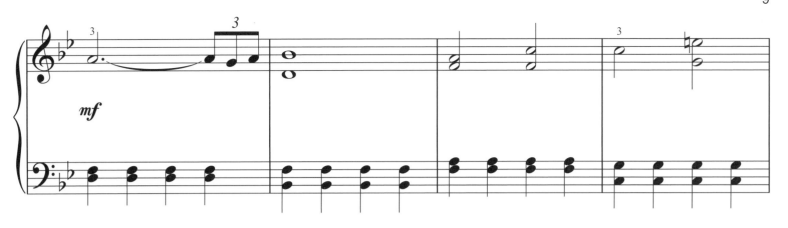

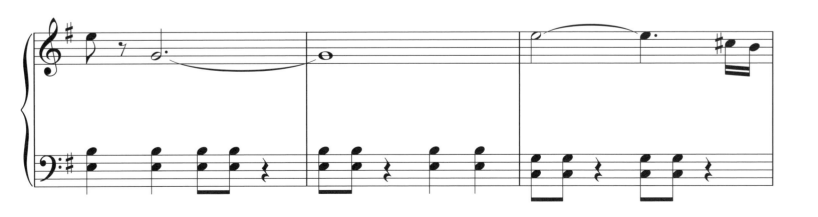

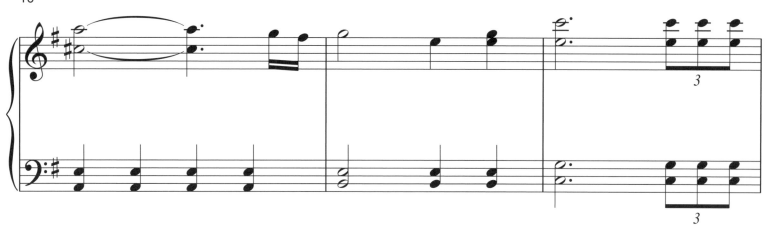

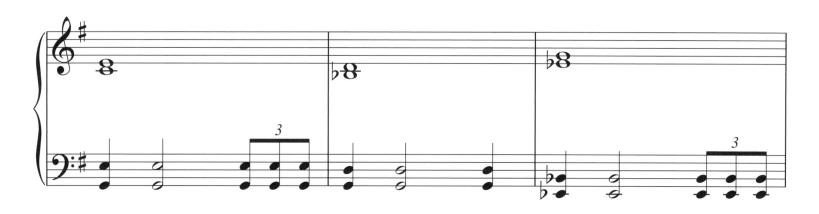

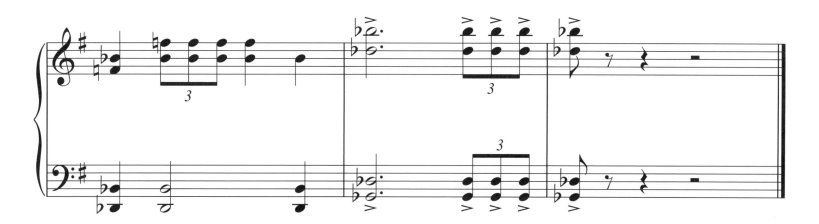

BACK TO THE FUTURE

from the Universal Motion Picture BACK TO THE FUTURE

By ALAN SILVESTRI

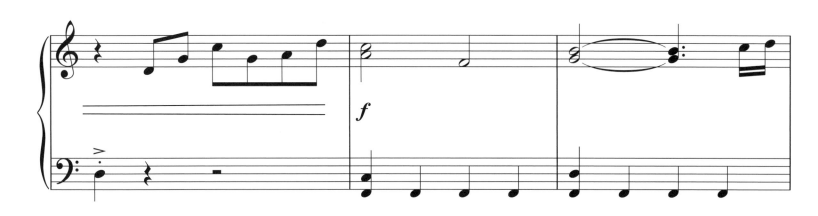

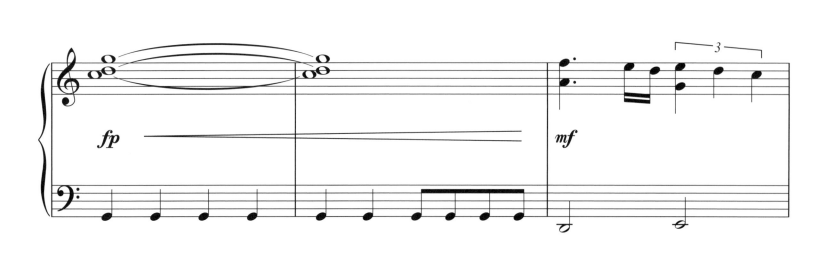

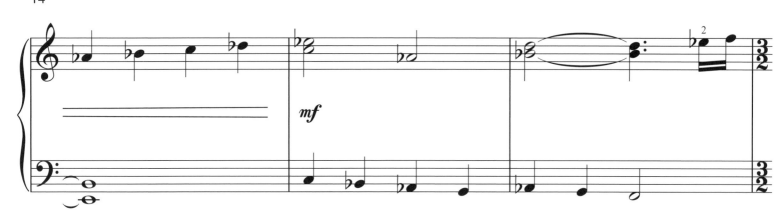

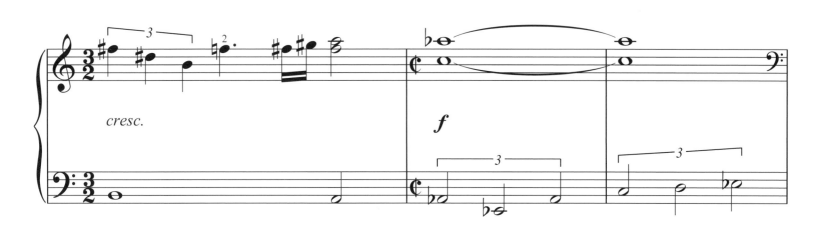

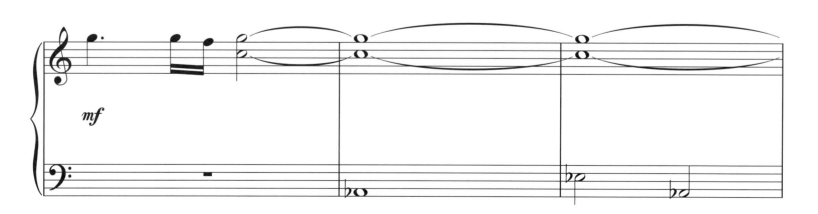

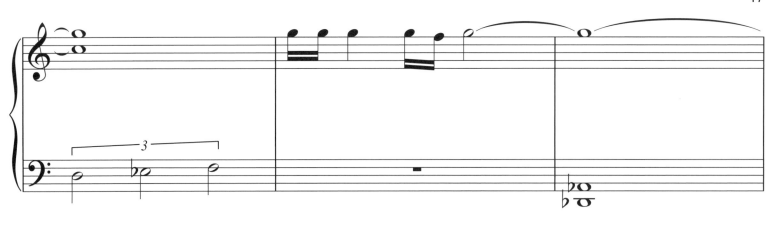

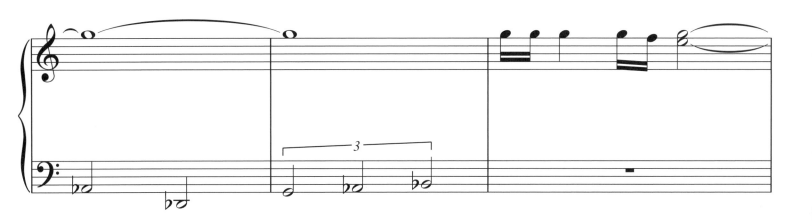

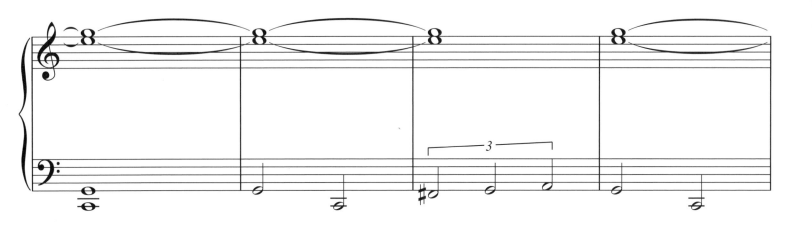

BATMAN THEME
from BATMAN

By DANNY ELFMAN

Slowly, freely

Vigorously

THE BATTLE
from the DreamWorks film GLADIATOR

Written by HANS ZIMMER

Broadly

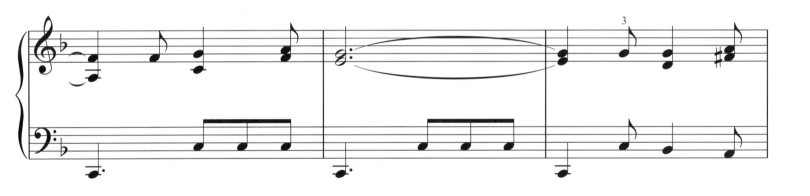

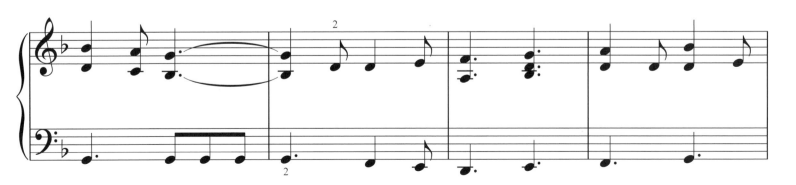

Slowly

mp

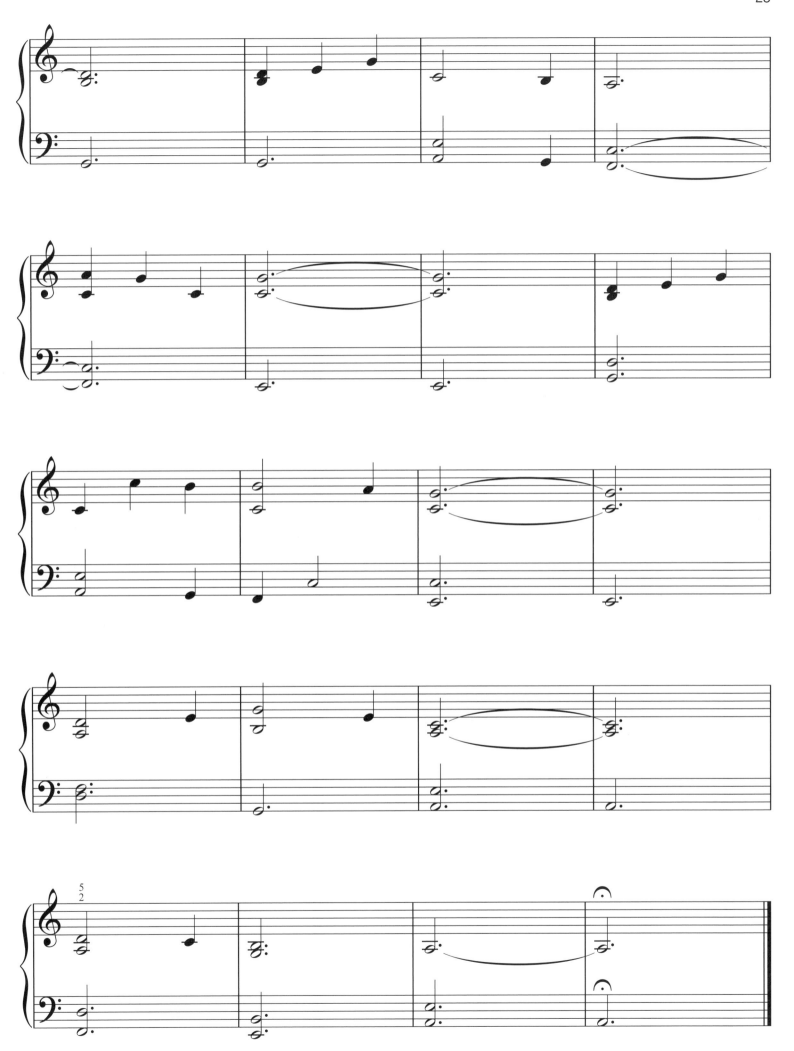

EVACUATING LONDON

from THE CHRONICLES OF NARNIA: THE LION, THE WITCH AND THE WARDROBE

Music by HARRY GREGSON-WILLIAMS

Slowly, expressively

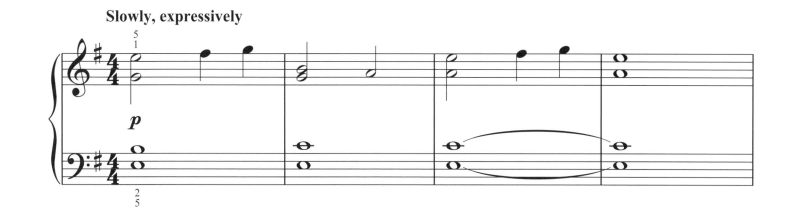

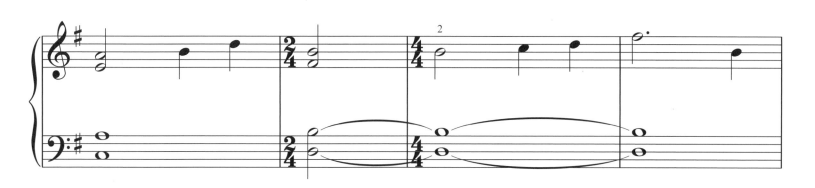

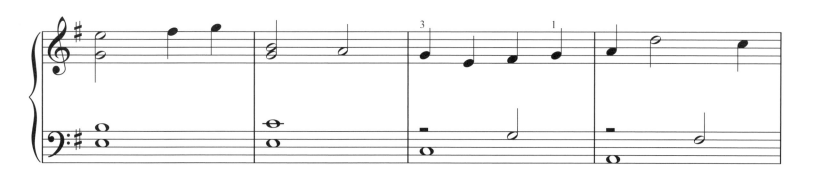

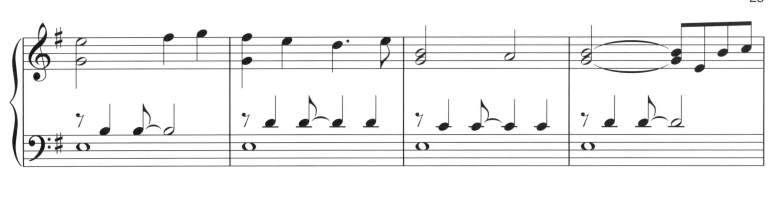

FANTASTIC BEASTS THEME

from FANTASTIC BEASTS: THE CRIMES OF GRINDELWALD

By JAMES NEWTON HOWARD

Mysteriously

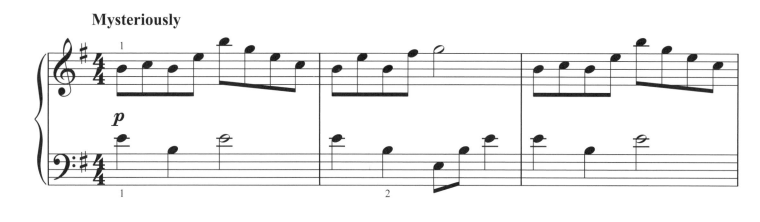

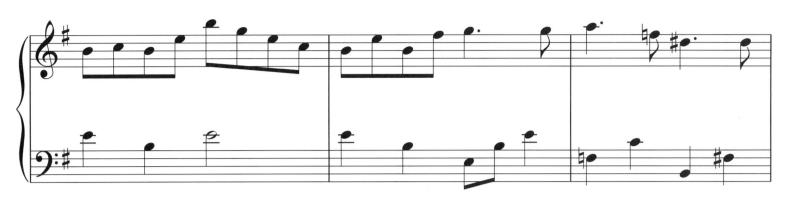

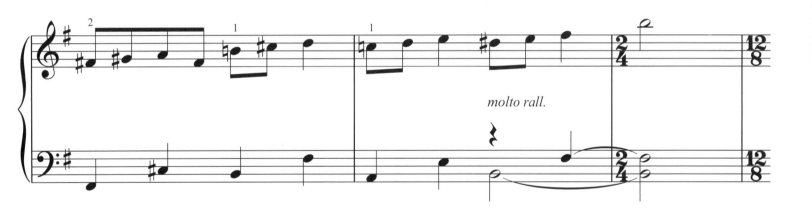

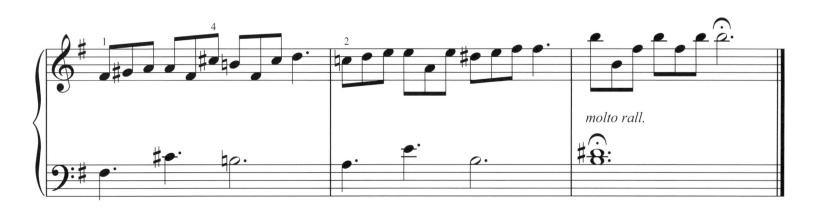

GOLLUM'S SONG
from THE LORD OF THE RINGS: THE TWO TOWERS

Words by FRAN WALSH
Music by HOWARD SHORE

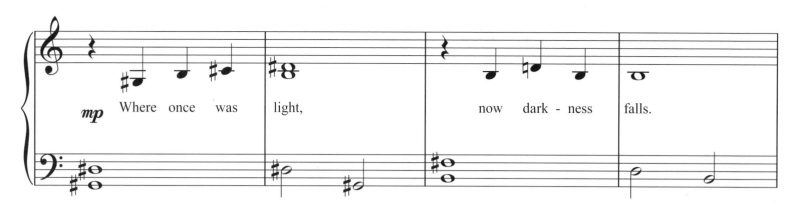

Where once was light, now dark - ness falls.

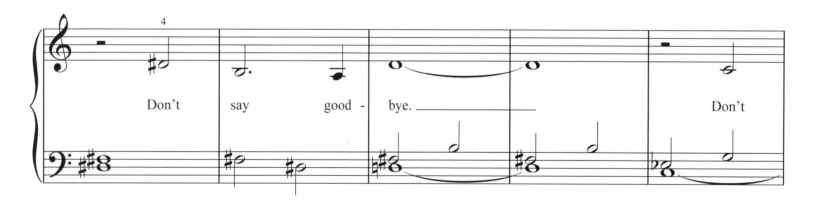

Where once was love, love is no more.

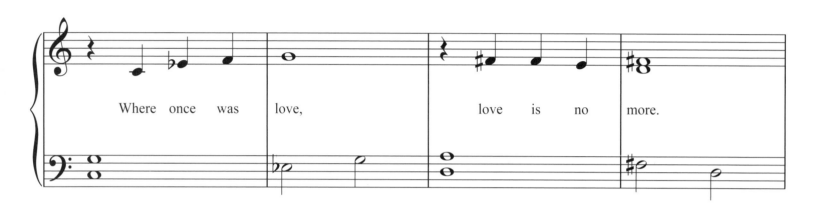

Don't say good - bye. _____ Don't

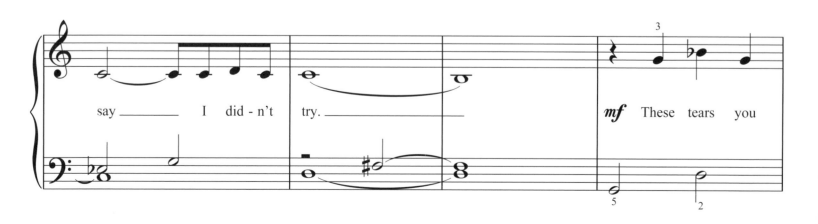

say _____ I did - n't try. _____ *mf* These tears you

cry are fall - ing rain, for all the

lies you told us, the hurt, the blame. And we will

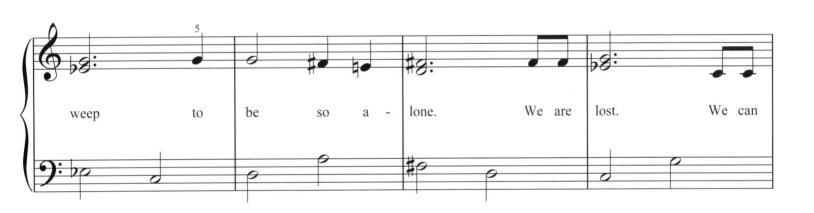

weep to be so a - lone. We are lost. We can

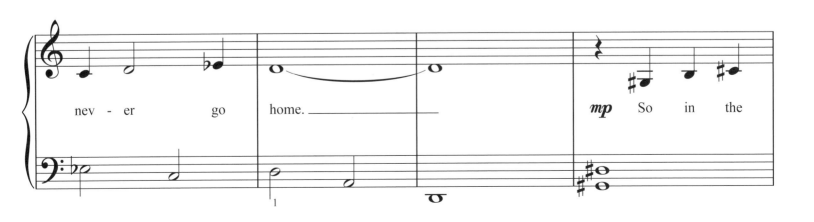

nev - er go home. _____ *mp* So in the

end   I'll   be   what   I   will   be.   No   loy - al

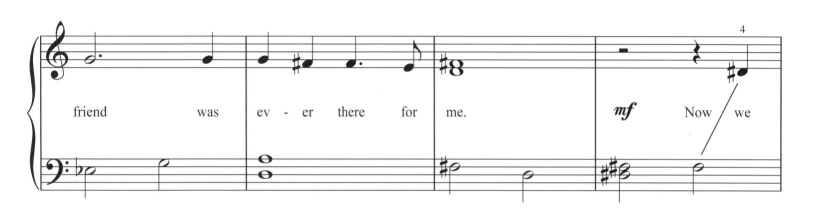

friend   was   ev - er   there   for   me.   *mf*   Now / we

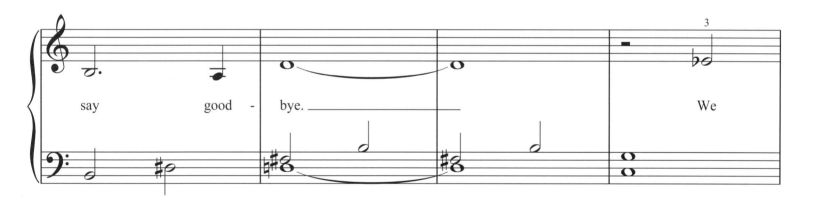

say   good - bye.   We

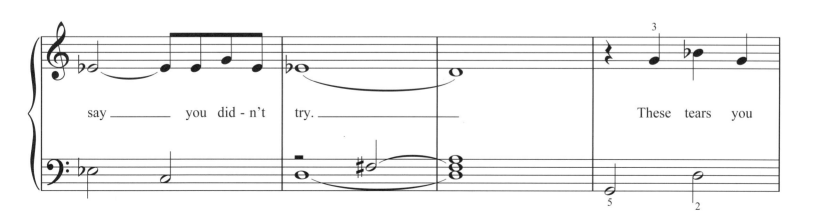

say _____ you did - n't   try.   These   tears   you

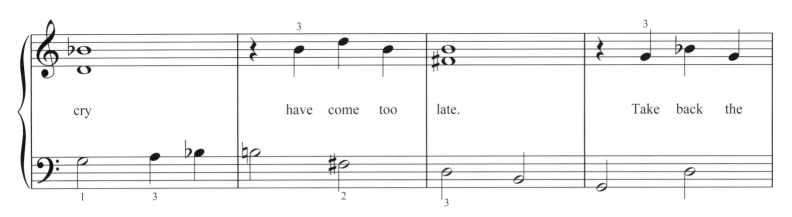

cry   have come too late.   Take back the

lies,   the hurt, the blame.   And you will

weep when you face the end a - lone.   You are lost.   You can

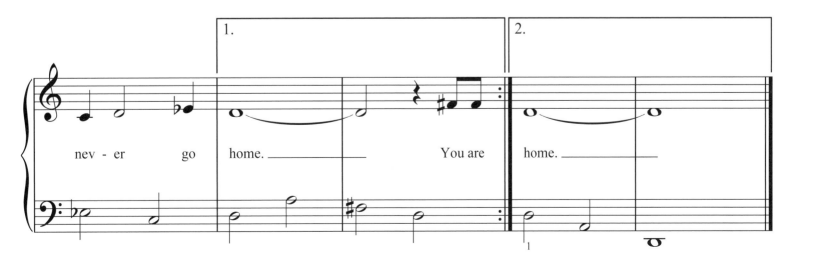

nev - er go home. _____ You are   home. _____

THE GOOD, THE BAD AND THE UGLY
(Main Title)
from THE GOOD, THE BAD AND THE UGLY

By ENNIO MORRICONE

Moderately fast

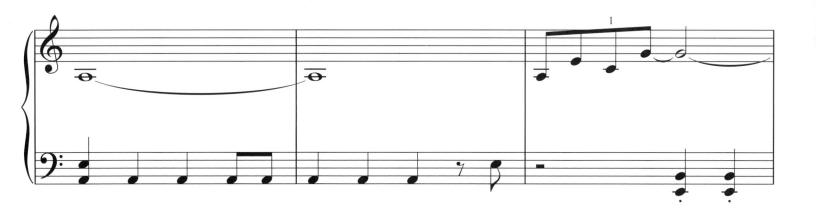

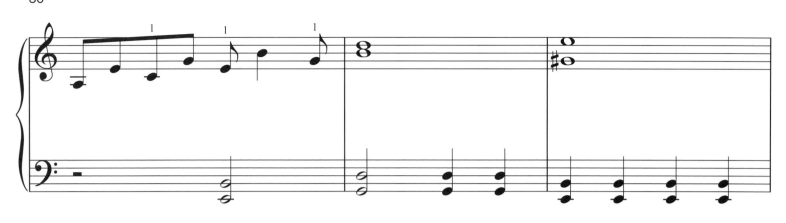

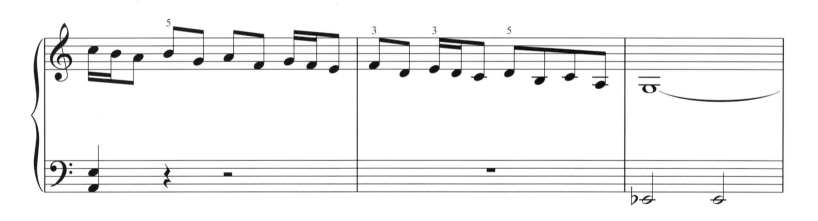

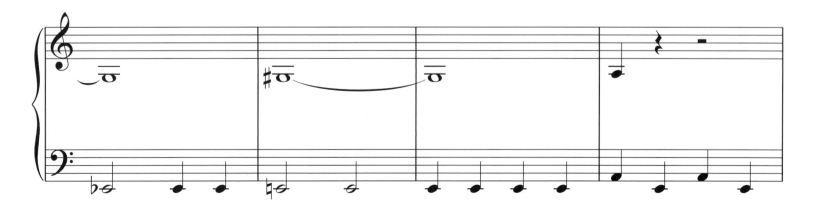

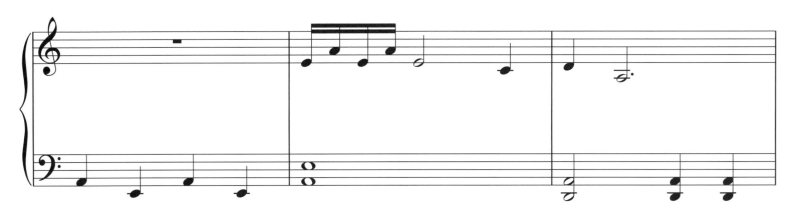

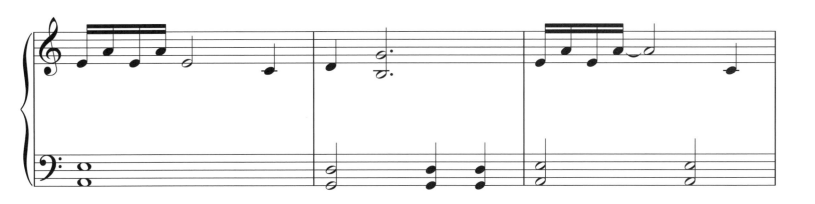

THE GREAT ESCAPE MARCH

from THE GREAT ESCAPE

Words by AL STILLMAN
Music by ELMER BERNSTEIN

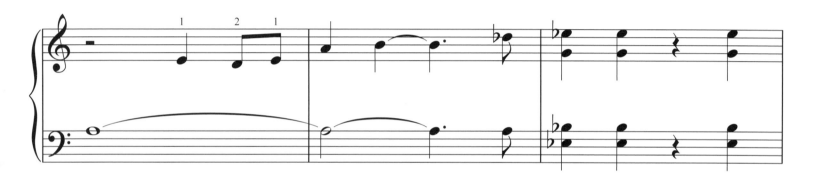

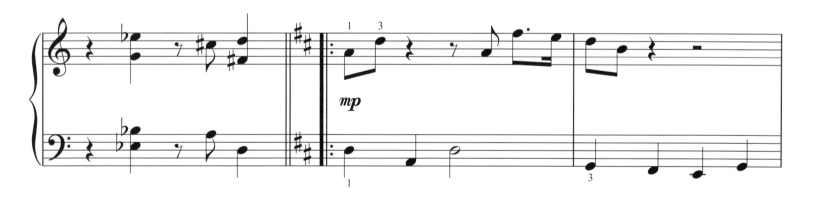

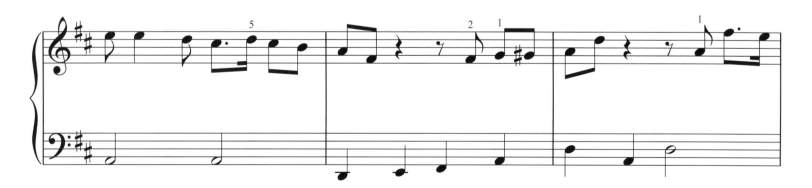

GUARDIANS INFERNO
from GUARDIANS OF THE GALAXY VOL. 2

Words and Music by JAMES GUNN
and TYLER BATES

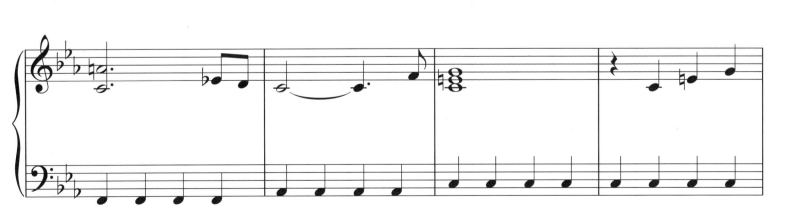

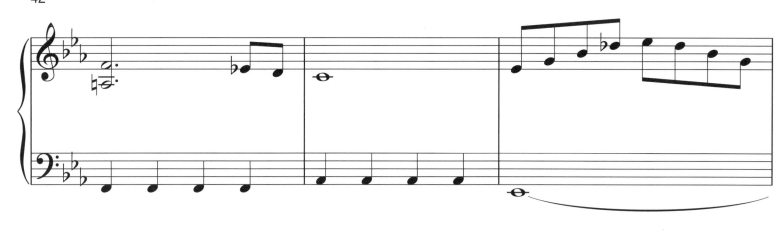

Solemn

HE'S A PIRATE
from PIRATES OF THE CARIBBEAN: THE CURSE OF THE BLACK PEARL

Written by HANS ZIMMER,
KLAUS BADELT and GEOFF ZANELLI

HEDWIG'S THEME

from the Motion Picture HARRY POTTER AND THE SORCERER'S STONE

By JOHN WILLIAMS

Misterioso

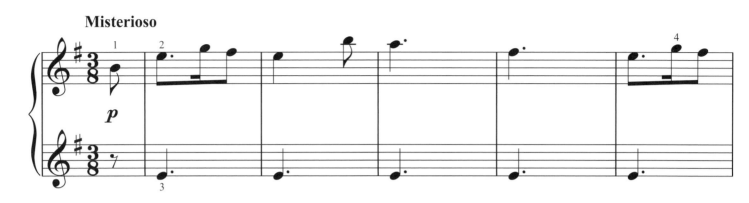

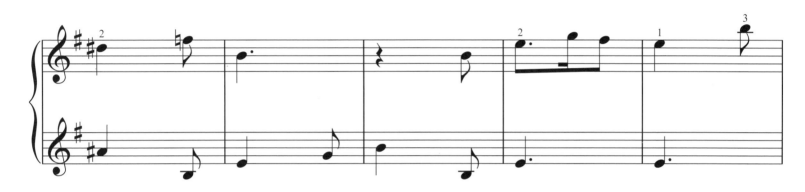

HUGO'S FATHER
from the Paramount Motion Picture HUGO

By HOWARD SHORE

HYMN TO THE FALLEN
from the Feature Film SAVING PRIVATE RYAN

Music by JOHN WILLIAMS

Slowly, reverently

I SEE YOU
(Theme from Avatar)
from the Twentieth Century Fox Motion Picture AVATAR

Lyrics by SIMON FRANGLEN,
JAMES HORNER and KUK HARRELL
Music by JAMES HORNER
and SIMON FRANGLEN

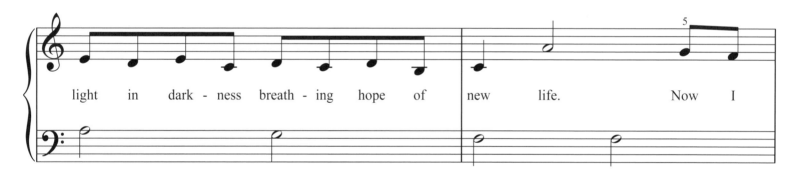

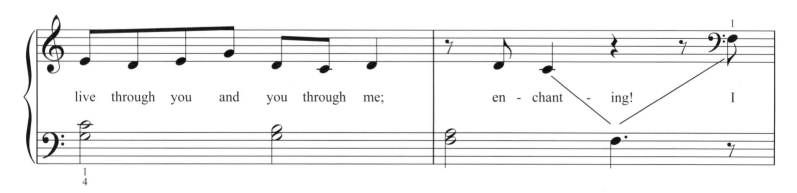

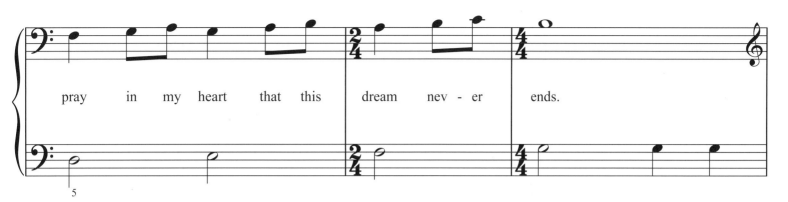

pray in my heart that this dream nev - er ends.

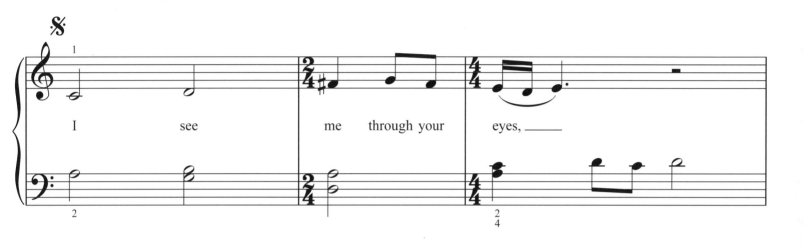

I see me through your eyes, _____

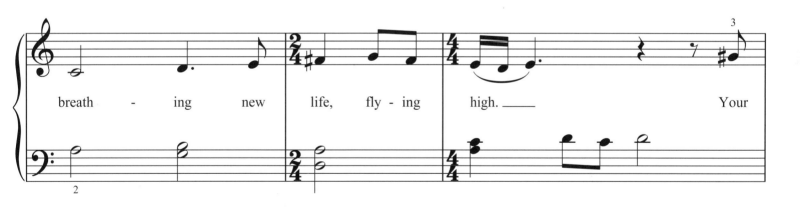

breath - ing new life, fly - ing high. _____ Your

To Coda ⊕

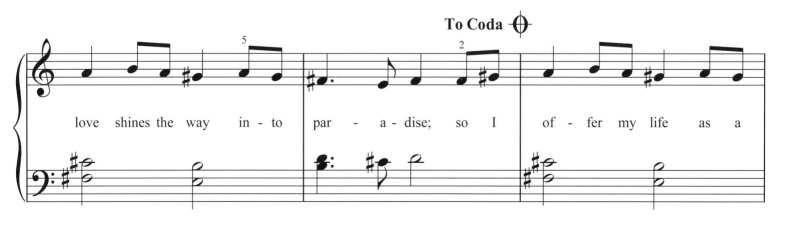

love shines the way in - to par - a - dise; so I of - fer my life as a

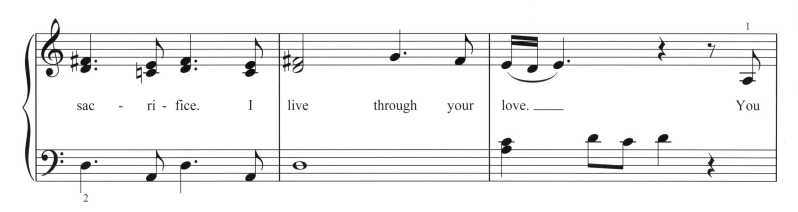

sac - ri - fice. I live through your love. _____ You

teach me how to see all that's beau - ti - ful; my

sens - es touch a world I've nev - er pic - tured. Now I give my hope to you; I sur -

D.S. al Coda

ren - der. I pray in my heart that this world nev - er ends.

of - fer my life, I _____ of - fer my love...

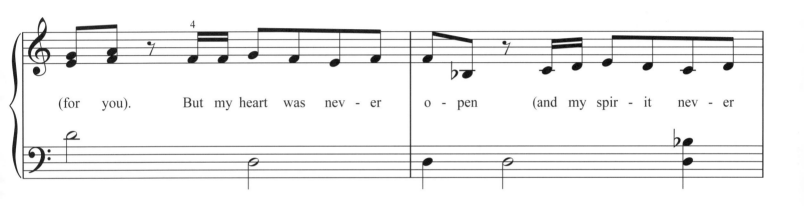

(for you). But my heart was nev - er o - pen (and my spir - it nev - er

free) to the world that you have shown me. _____

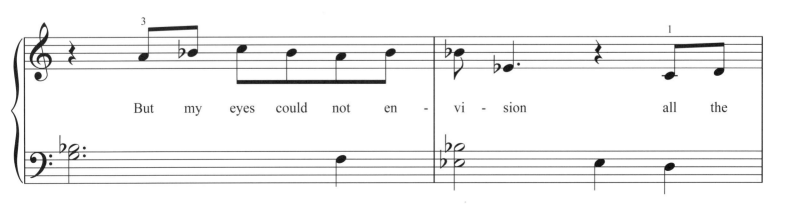

But my eyes could not en - vi - sion all the

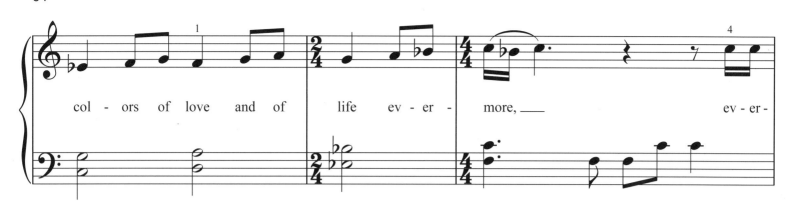

col - ors of love and of life ev - er - more, _____ ev - er-

more. _____ I see me _____ through your

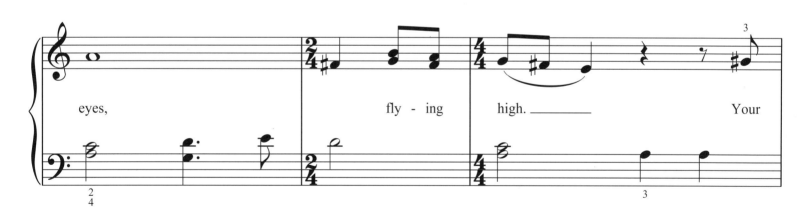

eyes, fly - ing high. _____ Your

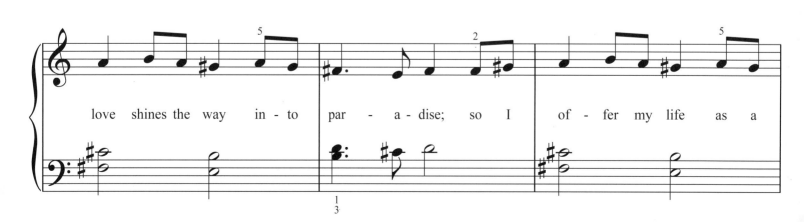

love shines the way in - to par - a - dise; so I of - fer my life as a

sac - ri - fice. I live through your love. I

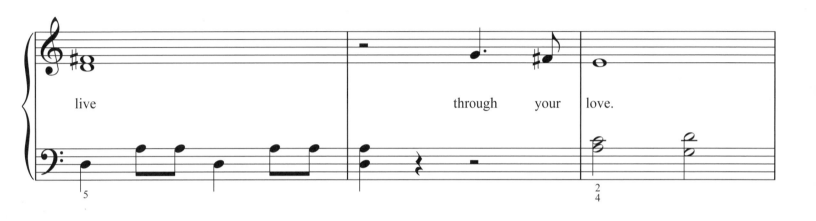

live through your love.

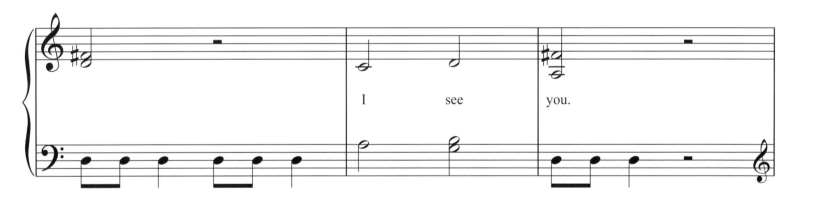

I see you.

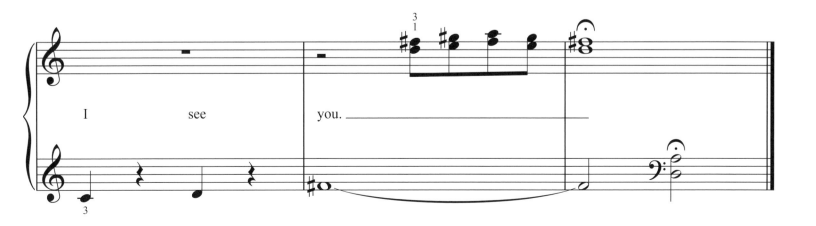

I see you.

THE IMPERIAL MARCH
(Darth Vader's Theme)
from STAR WARS: THE EMPIRE STRIKES BACK

Music by JOHN WILLIAMS

Ominously, in 2

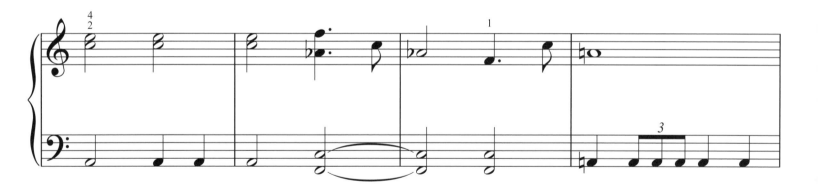

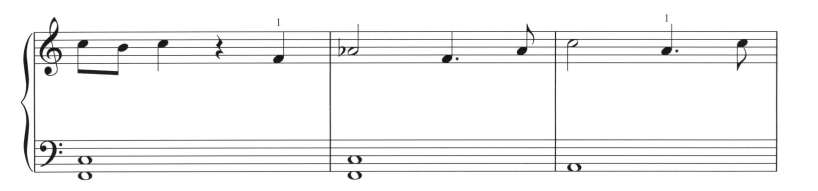

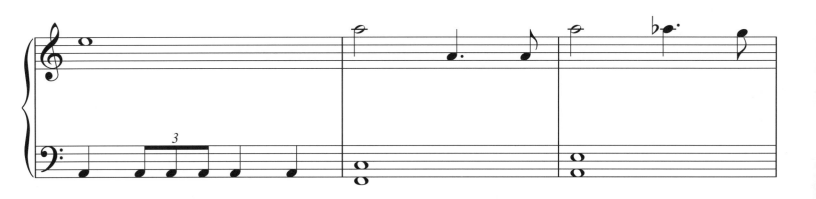

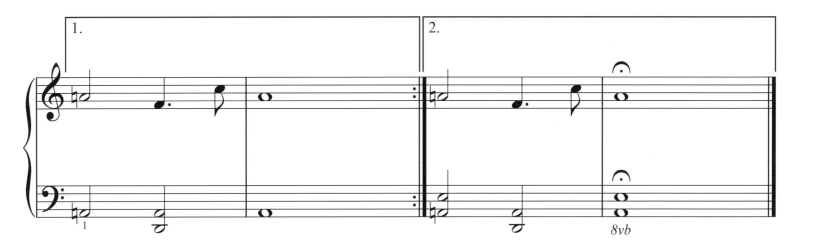

IRON MAN
from IRON MAN

By RAMIN DJAWADI

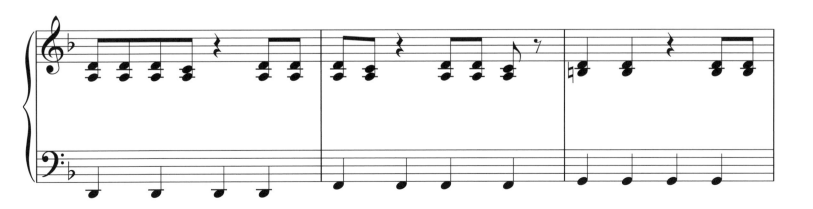

JAMES BOND THEME

from DR. NO

By MONTY NORMAN

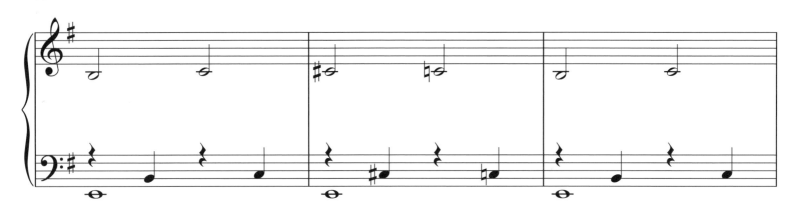

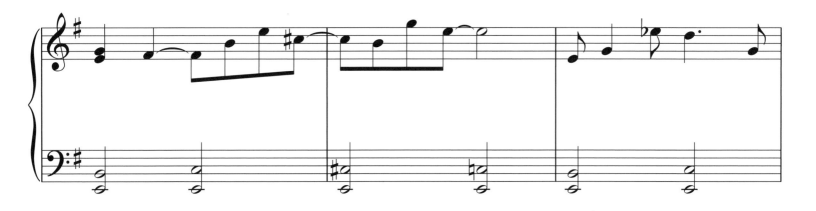

THEME FROM "JURASSIC PARK"

from the Universal Motion Picture JURASSIC PARK

Composed by JOHN WILLIAMS

THE MAGNIFICENT SEVEN

from THE MAGNIFICENT SEVEN

By ELMER BERNSTEIN

Moderately, with vigor

MISSION: IMPOSSIBLE THEME

from the Paramount Motion Picture MISSION: IMPOSSIBLE

By LALO SCHIFRIN

RAIDERS MARCH
from RAIDERS OF THE LOST ARK

Music by JOHN WILLIAMS

March tempo

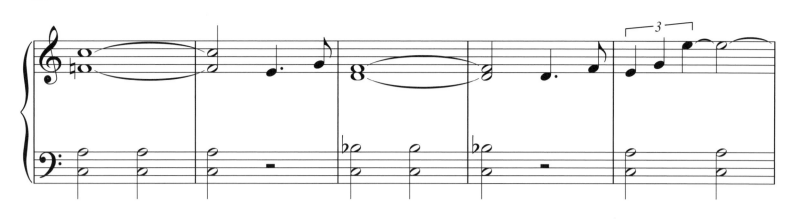

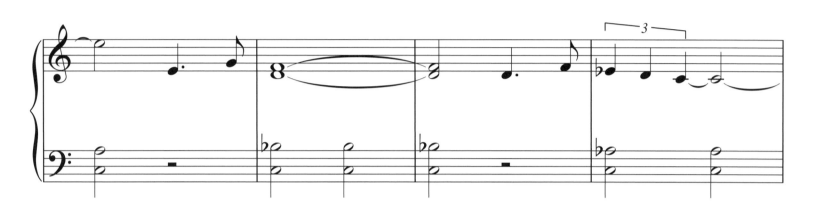

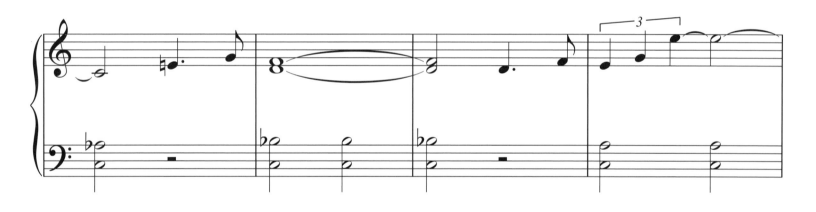

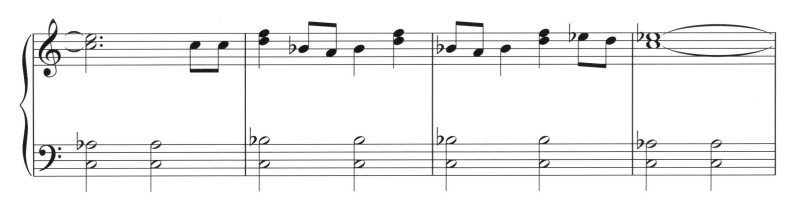

D.S. al Coda
(with repeat)

CODA

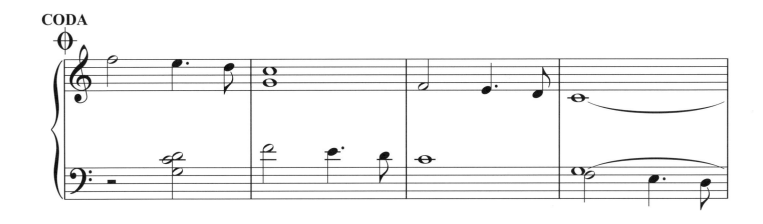

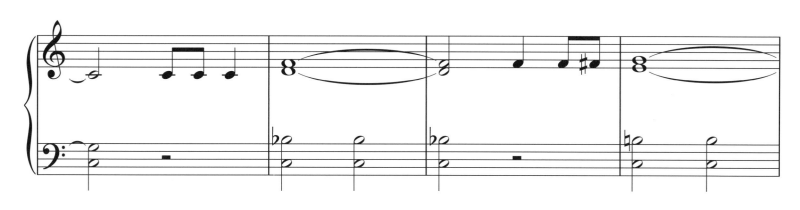

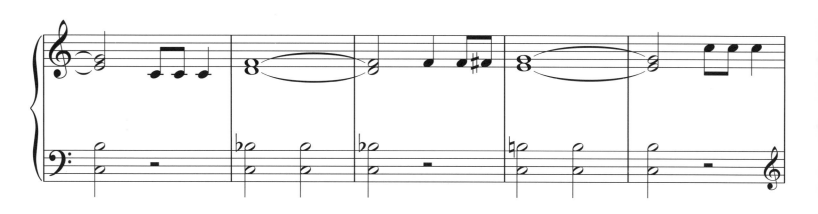

MISTY MOUNTAINS

from THE HOBBIT: AN UNEXPECTED JOURNEY

Words and Music by DAVID LONG,
JANET RODDICK, STEPHEN ROCHE,
DAVID DONALDSON, FRANCES WALSH
and PHILIPPA BOYENS

Slow and solemn

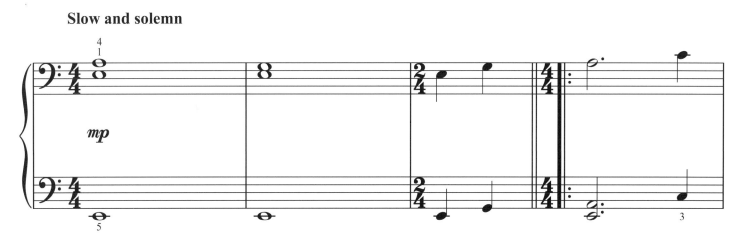

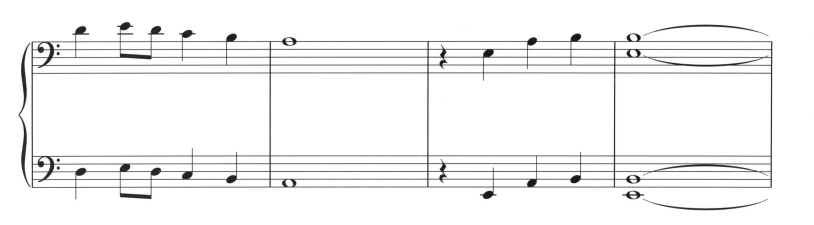

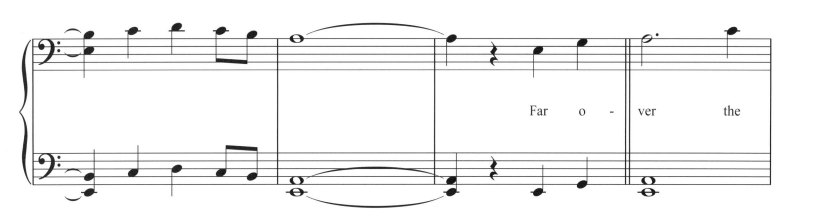

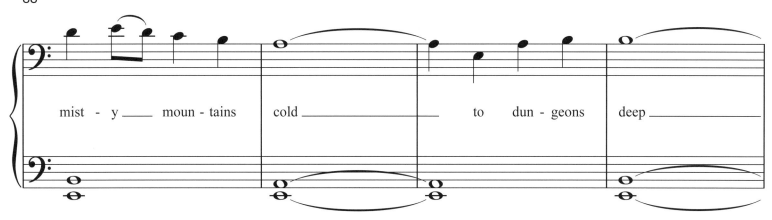

mist - y ___ moun - tains   cold ___   to dun - geons   deep ___

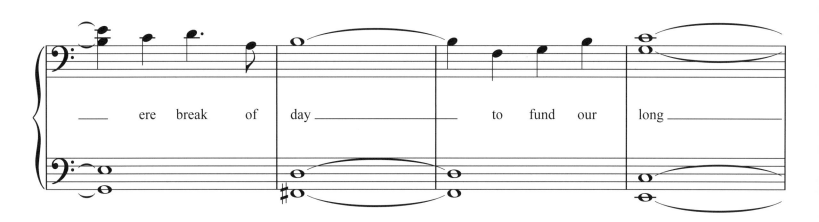

___   and   cav - erns ___   old, ___   we   must   a - way ___

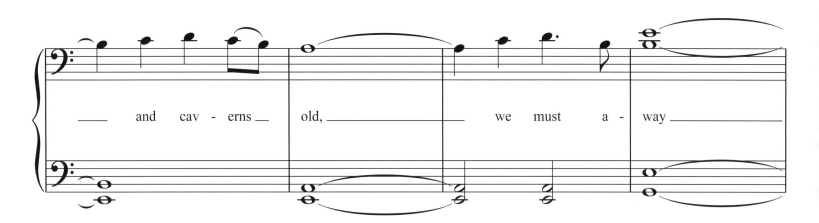

___   ere   break   of   day ___   to   fund   our   long ___

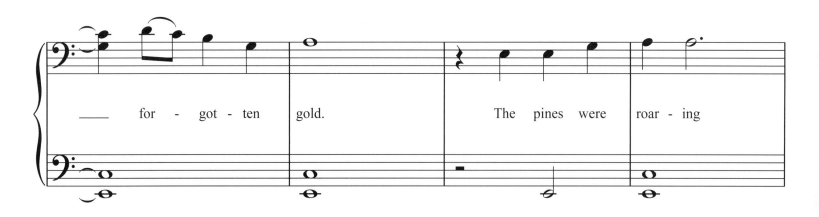

___   for - got - ten   gold.   The   pines   were   roar - ing

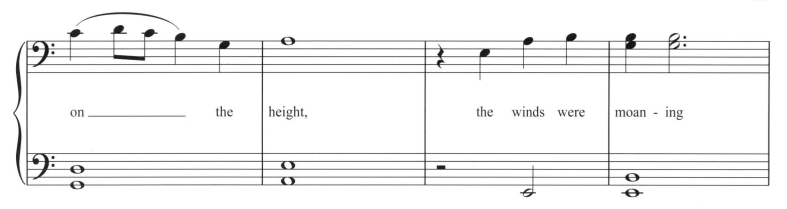

on _____ the height, the winds were moan - ing

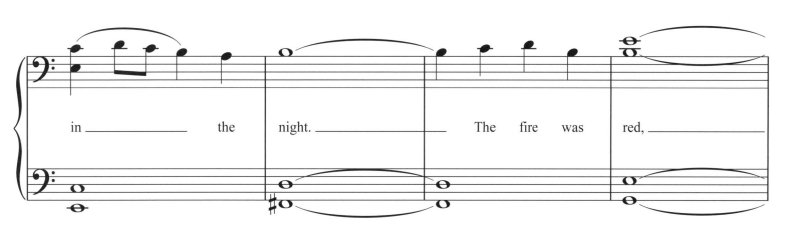

in _____ the night. _____ The fire was red, _____

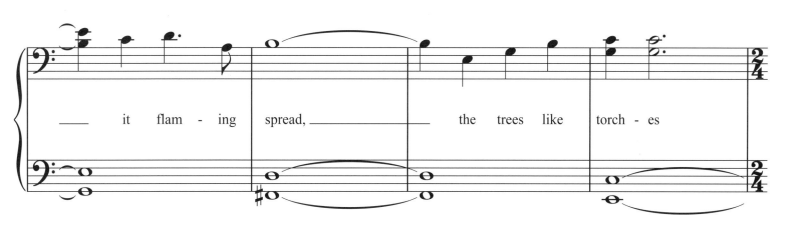

_____ it flam - ing spread, _____ the trees like torch - es

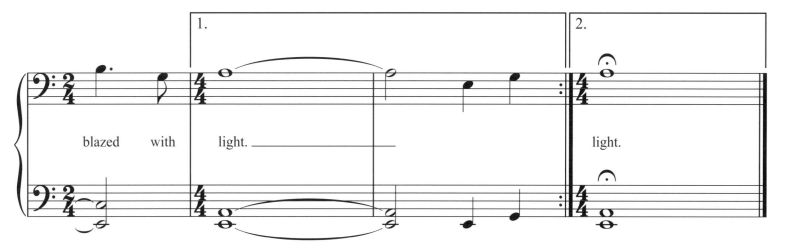

blazed with light. _____ light.

NEMO EGG
(Main Title)
from FINDING NEMO

By THOMAS NEWMAN

Slowly, gently

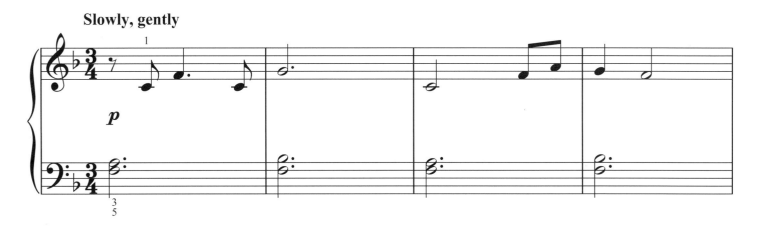

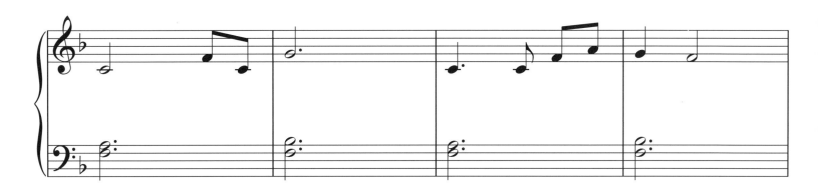

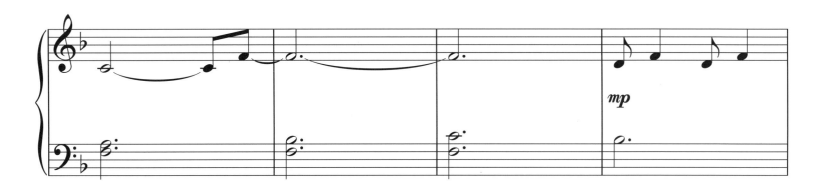

STAR TREK® THE MOTION PICTURE

Theme from the Paramount Motion Picture STAR TREK: THE MOTION PICTURE

Music by JERRY GOLDSMITH

Moderately fast March tempo

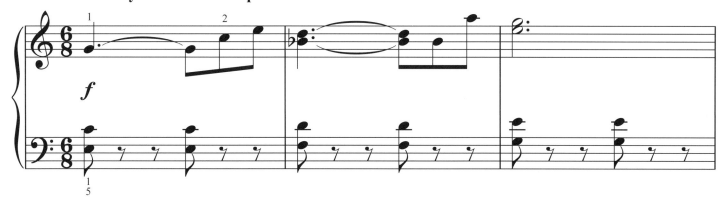

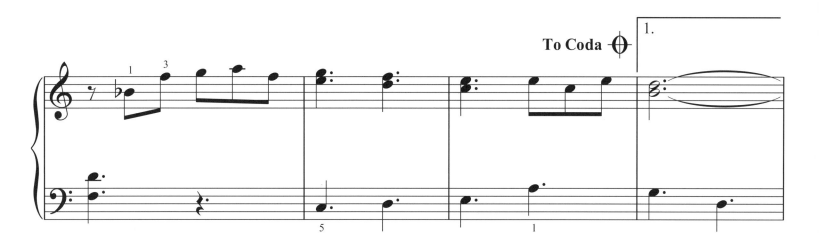

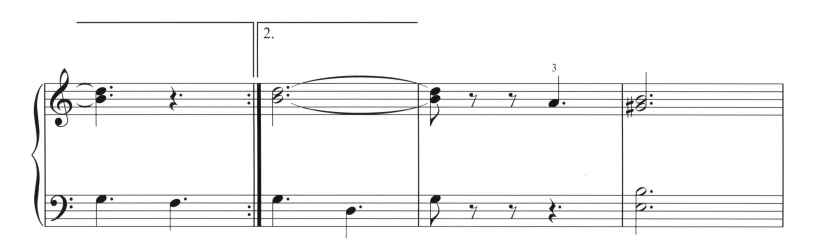

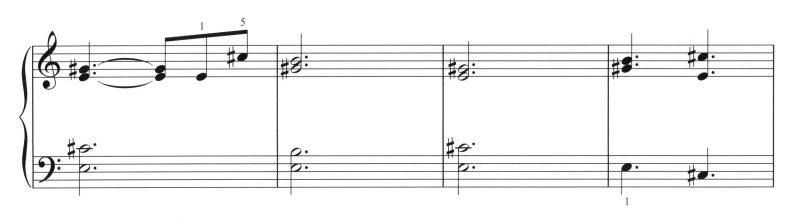

D.C. al Coda

CODA

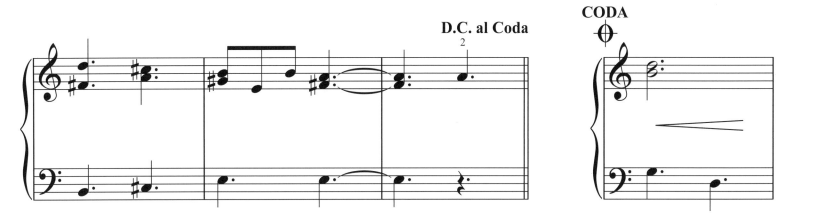

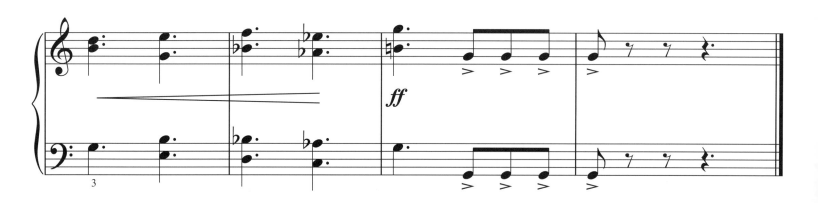

SPIDER-MAN: NO WAY HOME MAIN THEME

from SPIDER-MAN: NO WAY HOME

Written by MICHAEL G. GIACCHINO

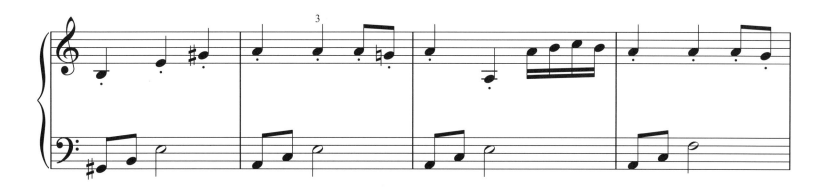

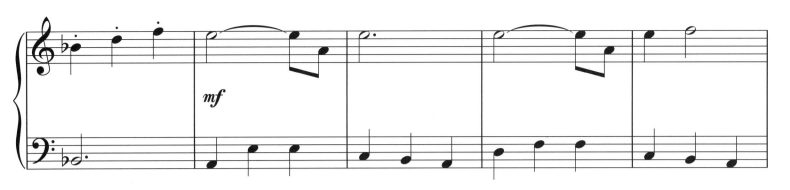

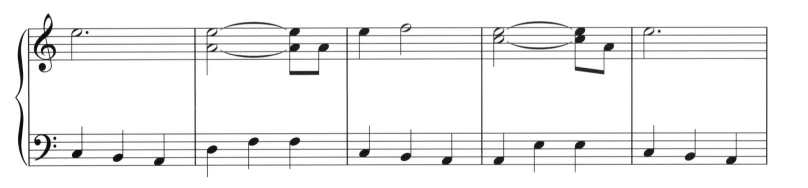

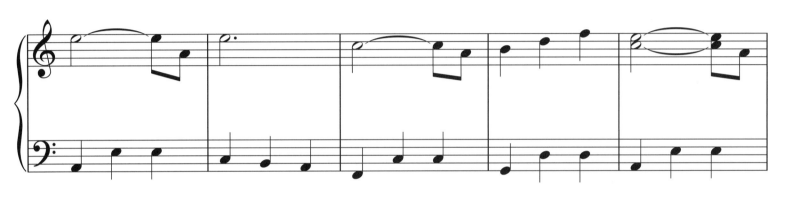

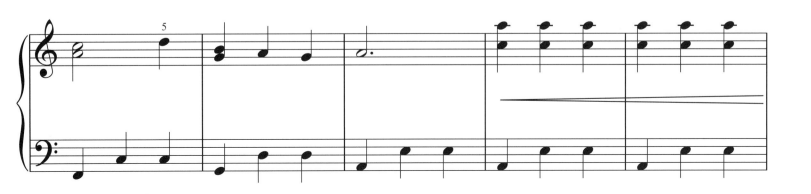

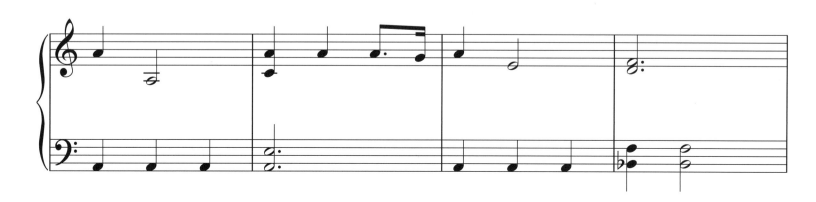

99

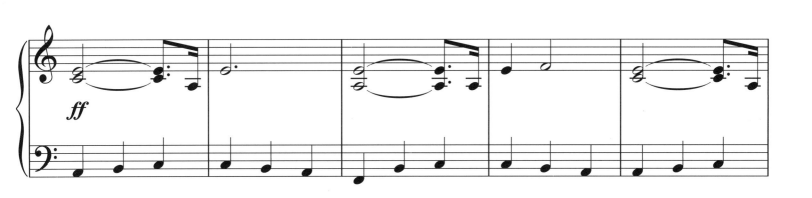

WAKANDA
from BLACK PANTHER

Music by LUDWIG GÖRANSSON

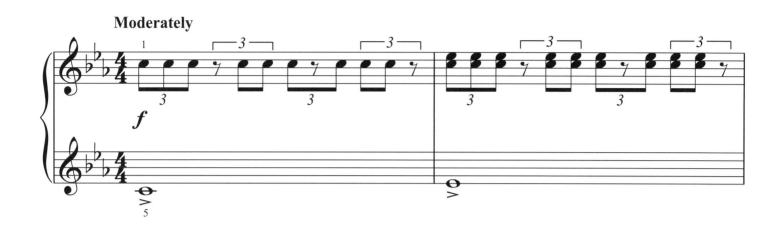

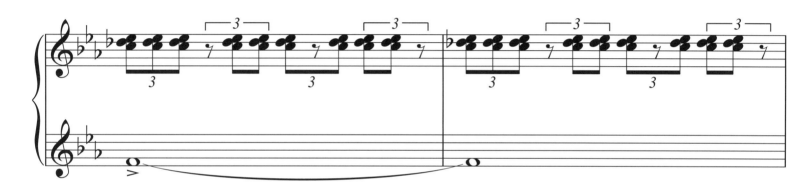

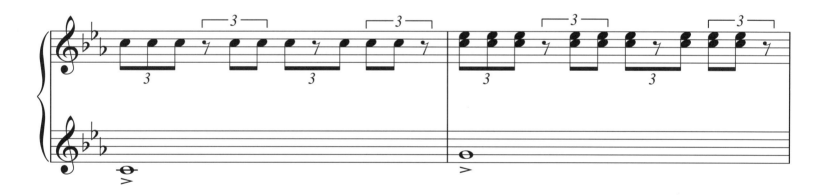

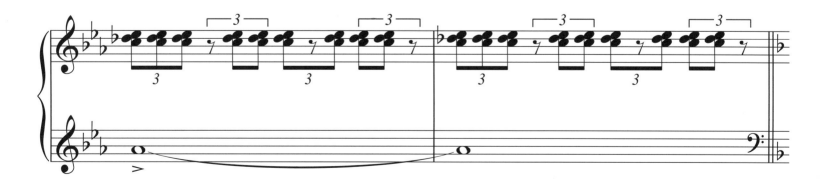

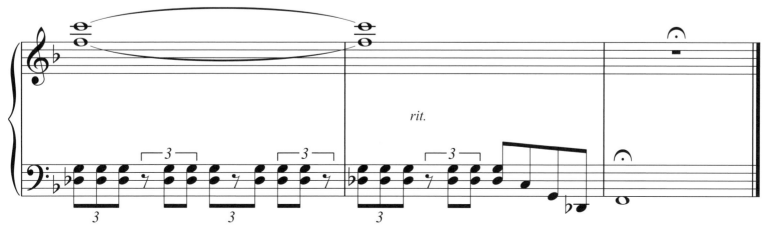

STAR WARS
(Main Theme)
from STAR WARS: A NEW HOPE

Music by JOHN WILLIAMS

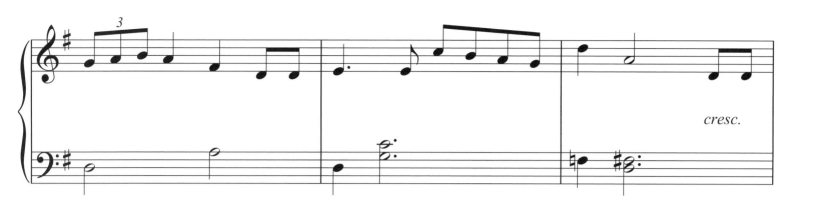

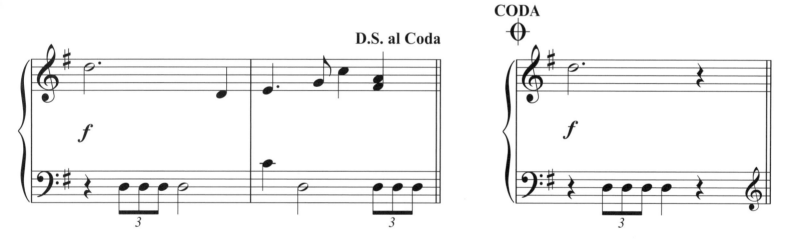

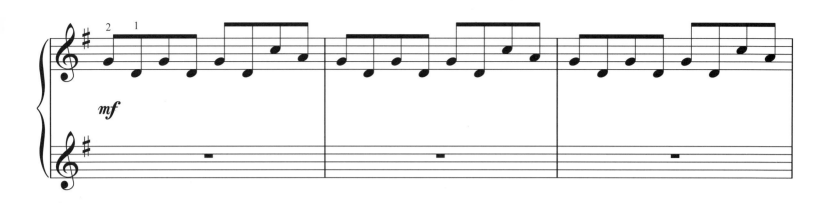

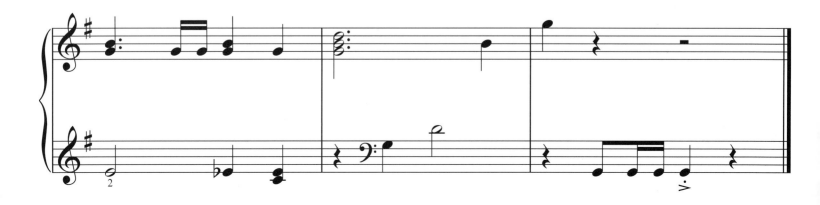